W9-CIB-395

BOOK-A-BRATIONS

Written & illustrated by Jan Grubb Philpot

Incentive Publications, Inc.
Nashville, Tennessee

Edited by Sally Sharpe

ISBN 0-86530-073-9

Table of Contents

LOVE THE BOOKS DAY

READING PROGRAMS

ABOUT THIS BOOK

BOOK-A-BRATIONS is a collection of activities and "celebrations" designed to actively involve students and teachers in books and reading. Each activity or celebration is accompanied by step-by-step instructions and reproducible announcements, awards, "parent-grams" and other useful materials to make the events easy to organize and direct.

Everything you need to publicize and promote the events is included in this book. Tips for utilizing school announcement systems and local newspapers and making radio spots will help you to "get the ball rolling" and solicit the support you need to make your event a success. Bulletin boards, bookmarks, reading records and other visual motivators also are included to stimulate and excite students.

Although BOOK-A-BRATIONS is written from a school librarian's point-of-view, all of the ideas presented in this book can be easily adapted by any classroom teacher, group or organization desiring to spotlight books and promote reading.

These exciting "book-a-brations" will spread reading enthusiasm throughout the entire school. Students of all ages will enjoy becoming "involved" in literature and will subsequently develop a reading curiosity that will open the door to many wonderful and rewarding experiences.

Radio spots are a terrific way to advertise your book-a-brations, to involve students, and to let parents and the community know that you are on your toes!

- Radio stations provide this service free of charge. Simply call a local station and explain the upcoming event. (Ask whether they prefer you to use a cassette or reel-to-reel tape.) Request that they air the spot periodically during the chosen week.

- Send an announcement to each classroom asking the class to send a representative to the media center for taping on the chosen day (page ix). The representative may be chosen by the teacher or the class. Drawing names is often a good way to do this. Be sure to send a copy of the spot with the announcement so that the chosen representative may practice before the taping.

  Important: Keep the spot short and to the point. This will eliminate stumbling and stuttering. Even kindergarteners who cannot read can memorize a short spot!

  Sample spot:

  Hi! My name is ________________ and I'm in ____________________________'s class at ____________________________. Our library is sponsoring ____________________________ on ________________________ in honor of books and reading. We'd like to ask parents to encourage their children to read for the fun of it!

- Give a participation bookmark to each student who makes a spot. Send a parent-gram (page ix) home with each student so that moms and dads will know where and when to "tune in"!

Participation Bookmark

The media center is celebrating ______________________________.
Each class may choose one representative to read the announcement below for a radio spot to publicize the event.

The representative should report to the media center at ________ (time) on ______________ (date) for taping.

Announcements will air on ___________ (station) the week of ____________ (date).

Announcement:

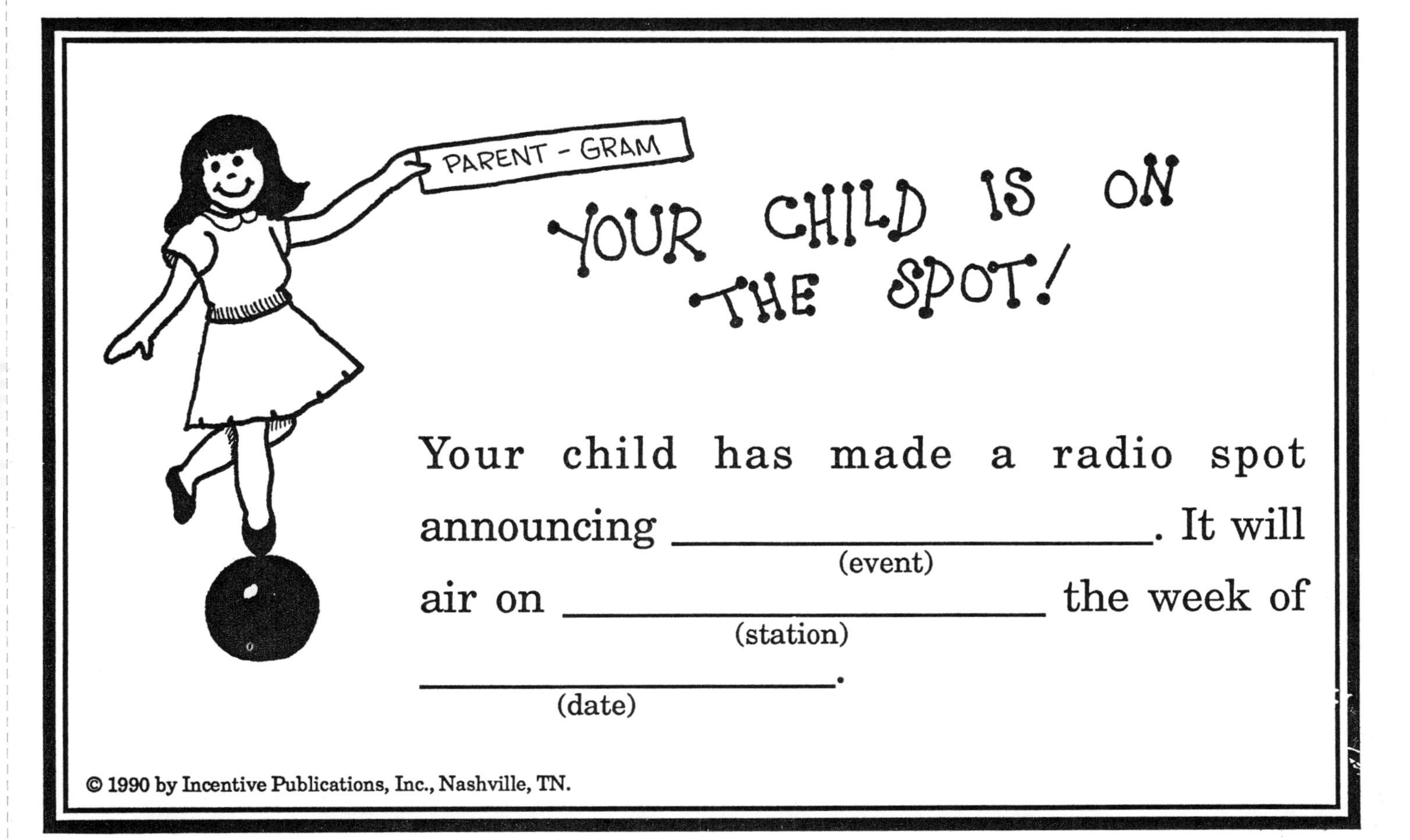

Your child has made a radio spot announcing ______________________ (event). It will air on ______________________ (station) the week of ____________________ (date).

GHOST STORY
JAMBOREE
A STUDENT STORYTELLING
BOOK-A-BRATION!

Ghost Story Jamboree is an activity that children dearly love and a great way to get students involved in storytelling!

PLANNING & ORGANIZATION

1. Send a notice to every classroom announcing the Ghost Story Jamboree (see page 14). The notice will explain that each classroom is to host its own storytelling session and select the best storyteller. The chosen storyteller is to represent the class in the Ghost Story Jamboree.

2. Prepare your students for storytelling by telling stories during each class' library period. (Be sure the students understand the difference between storytelling and book reporting!) Some good resources include:

Audiovisual
Storytelling Series On Video
(H.W. Wilson Co., 1987)

Records
"Hairy Man & Other Wild Tales"
by David Holt (High Windy, 1981)

"Taily Bone & Other Strange Tales"
by David Holt (High Windy, 1985)

"Chillers"
by Connie Regan & Barbara Freeman (The Folktellers), (Mama-T, 1983)

"Tales For Scary Times"
by Jackie Torrence (Earwig, 1985)

"Storytelling: The National Festival"
National Assoc. for the Preservation & Perpetuation of Storytelling (Jonesborough, TN, 1983)

"Graveyard Tales"
National Assoc. for the Preservation & Perpetuation of Storytelling (Jonesborough, TN, 1984)

3. Set up a display of Halloween books for the students to use as resources. Be sure to explain that the story does not have to come from a book, but may be a family story or an original tale. Encourage the young storytellers to be creative in their storytelling by using costumes, props and/or sound effects.

4. Use the certificate on page 17 for honoring the winners and the bookmark on page 18 for recognizing all participants. (You may award prizes if you wish.)

YOU WERE SPOOK-TACULAR IN THE GHOST STORY JAMBOREE!

Congratulations, ________;
for placing ____ in our story telling contest on ________.

____
Signed

5. Be sure to secure judges ahead of time. It is generally best to select judges that are not from your school. Good choices include children's literature instructors, librarians in your district, or public librarians. Be sure to send thank-you's to the judges (see page 18).

6. This event is especially nice if you have a video camera and a closed circuit T.V. system. Students are not nearly as nervous when looking into a camera as they might be when looking into a sea of faces. The videotape can be viewed and reviewed by the judges and can be aired on closed circuit T.V. for the entire school. Or, have the storytellers perform in a gym or auditorium. If this is not possible, have the representatives tell their stories to the panel of judges and then make visits to individual classrooms.

7. Don't forget the media! Local newspapers will want pictures of the storytellers in full costume.

HELPFUL HINTS

- Have a "Vincent Vampire" (or "Vincetta Vampire") to be your master of ceremonies! (Use a student or library aide!)

- Play sound effects and/or "spooky" music in the background while the storytellers tell their tales.

- Experiment with the lighting and color controls on the video camera to get some "weird" effects!

Take part in the Ghost Story Jamboree! Here's how:

Host a ghost storytelling contest in your room the week of ____________________. Vote on a winner and send the name of the winner to the media center.

Winners report to the media center on ____________________ for:

____ performance for judges.
____ videotaping.
____ instructions for sharing their stories with the school.

Storytellers are encouraged to perform in costume and to use props, sound effects, etc.

Plans for sharing the stories with the school:

PARENT - GRAM
BOO-ti-ful news!
Your child, ________,
has been selected
by his/her class to perform
in the Media Center's
GHOST STORY JAMBOREE!
You are invited to watch:
Date ________ Time ______ Place ________
© 1990 by Incentive Publications, Inc., Nashville, TN.

YOU ARE
INVITED TO
VIEW THE
GHOST STORY
JAMBOREE!
DATE ________
TIME ________
PLACE ________
© 1990 by Incentive Publications, Inc., Nashville, TN.

GHOST STORY JAMBOREE JUDGE'S SHEET

Student ____________________ Homeroom ____________________

	Poor		Good		Excellent
1. Eye contact, facial expression	1	2	3	4	5
2. Voice expression	1	2	3	4	5
3. Creativity of presentation (Use of props, sound effects, costumes, etc.)	1	2	3	4	5
4. Story selection	1	2	3	4	5
5. Overall effect	1	2	3	4	5

Total Points: _________

Additional Comments:

YOU WERE
SPOOK-
TACULAR
IN THE
GHOST STORY
JAMBOREE!
Congratulations, ________,
for placing ___ in our story-
telling contest on ________.
Signed

THANKS for
participating
in the
GHOST
STORY
JAMBOREE
on ____.
You did a
BOO-ti-ful
JOB!
© 1990 by Incentive Publications, Inc.,
Nashville, TN.

You sure GHOST
to a lot of
trouble for us–
THANKS for judging our
GHOST STORY JAMBOREE.
You did a BOO-ti-ful
JOB!
© 1990 by Incentive Publications, Inc., Nashville, TN.

PARADE OUT
THE SKY IS FALLING!
THE BOOKS!

A BOOK PARADE is a good way to spotlight books and let students "strut" their creativity. Classrooms are invited to choose a book theme and to design an entry for the parade.

WHEN & WHERE

The book parade is a good year-end activity. The school playground is a good location for the parade. Classes and/or students who choose not to participate can line the outskirts of the chosen area to form a pathway for the parade. Have each float entry pass in front of the observers and then take its place at the end of the line so that the children in that class can watch the rest of the parade.

Organization is the key to success and to making this event one that everyone looks forward to annually. . . so read on. . . .

PLANNING & ORGANIZATION

1. Be sure to clear the event with your principal. You'll have more success if you are able to show him or her that you are organized!

2. Send an announcement to every classroom (see page 25). This is an exciting activity that everyone enjoys and one that has a way of becoming an annual event. At first, however, teachers will ask you for ideas and suggestions for possible entries. The ideas below and on the next page are a few good ideas for starters. . .

• *Hansel and Gretel*

Use cardboard boxes and a child's wagon to create a "gingerbread" house on wheels. Have the children glue cookies and candy on the house. Let Hansel, Gretel and the witch accompany the float.

• *Where the Wild Things Are*

Turn a child's wagon into a "sailboat" (use cardboard). Let Max, dressed in his wolf suit, accompany the float. The rest of the class can be "wild things" by wearing paper bag masks.

• *The Wizard of Oz*

Let the Scarecrow, Tin Man and Lion pull Dorothy in a wagon as "Somewhere Over the Rainbow" plays in the background. (Hint: Wrap the arms and legs of the Tin Man in aluminum foil.)

• *Little House in the Big Woods*

Have the Ingalls family accompany a "log cabin" on wheels (cardboard box on a child's wagon).

• *Make Way for Ducklings*

Have a policeman blow a whistle and "make way" for a string of little "ducks."

• *Millions of Cats*

Paint noses and whiskers on the students and give them paper ears and tails to complete their cat costumes. Have the "cats" follow a "little old man."

• Nonfiction abounds with ideas!

Make cardboard spaceships and "spacepersons" for books in the 600's, have the children wear "native" costumes for books about various countries, etc.

3. Explain to the teachers the different ways that floats can be made (refer to the ideas on pages 21 and 22). Many entries, however, are just as effective without a "float" (such as the ideas for *Millions of Cats* and *Make Way for Ducklings*). After you get the "wheels in motion," you'll be surprised just how creative the students and teachers can be! Stress that the students are to do the majority of the work involved in preparing the entries. Teachers may provide ideas, patterns, supervision, etc.

4. One child should be selected from each classroom to give a short synopsis of the chosen book over the loudspeaker as the class' entry passes before the crowd.

Hint: Playing music in the background adds a lot to the effectiveness of an entry. Tell the teachers who wish to use music to ask the child giving the story synopsis to hand the person in charge a tape at the appropriate time.

5. Post a sign-up sheet for entries in a convenient place. The faculty lounge is a good place. Each teacher should designate the book his or her class has chosen. This will generate interest as well as help you plan for the parade. (One class per title!)

6. Secure judges. It is preferable to have three judges (in order to break ties) who are not from your school and who are knowledgeable about children's books (i.e. district librarians, public librarians, library supervisors, etc.).

Type a list of the books to be represented and include a one-paragraph summary of each book. Give a copy of the list to each judge in advance.

7. You will need the following items: a cassette tape player, a public announcement system, and chairs for the judges. You also may want to ask someone to take pictures or to videotape the parade!

8. Prepare the awards. Use the certificate on page 26 to make awards for various categories. Because the entries will be so varied, use the following or similar categories:

Most Original or Most Creative
Most Beautiful
Best Representation of Book Theme

Give all of the other entries a participation award (page 27).

9. Publicize the event! This activity generates a great deal of interest and is rather impressive. Call your local newspaper and ask a reporter and/or a photographer to attend the parade.

10. On the day of the parade. . .

- Be sure you have all of your materials (tape player, PA system, chairs for the judges, awards, camera).

- Call for the entries one at a time on the school intercom. Position each class in a line to one side of the PA system.

- Call for the rest of the classes and instruct them to position themselves close together on the outskirts of the playground. Once the teachers understand where their classes are supposed to be, they can supervise the positioning of the students. (Note: If the playground is paved, it is a good idea to have the students sit.)

- Announce the beginning of "Parade Out The Books." Make your opening remarks and introduce the judges.

- Announce the first entry, naming the class and its chosen book. Then, hand the microphone to the student chosen to give the story synopsis. (Remind the student to speak loudly!)

- If music is to accompany the entry, ask the student for the tape and get ready to start the music!

- After introducing the entry, motion the class to parade in front of the observers. Once the class has completed its "parade," the students may take their places at the end of the line to view the rest of the parade.

  Hint: It is a good idea to allow each entry to finish its "parade" before motioning another class to begin, unless there are a large number of entries.

- After the parade is over, remind the students that everyone who participated is a winner! At this time, turn the program over to the judges. As they announce the winners, present the classes with their awards. Remember to give all participating classes participation awards (see page 27) once the winners have been announced.

- You've done it! And wasn't it spectacular? Don't forget to send thank-you's to the judges (see page 27)!

Suggestion: You may want to have a "run-through" rehearsal (no costumes or props!) before the day of the parade.

We're **Parading Out The Books** on ______________________________ at
________________________!
(date)
(time)

Here's how classes can participate:

Choose a favorite book and . . .

Design a parade entry for the book. The entry can be, but is not limited to, a float built by the students on a child's wagon. Your entry may consist of students wearing costumes and/or carrying props. You may have background music and/or sound effects. (One class per book!)

One student should be selected to give a short synopsis of the book prior to the presentation.

The parade will be held at ________________________________.
(place)

Awards will be given for these categories: ______________________________

____.

Sign up by ____________________ on the sheet in the ____________________.
(date) (place)

CONGRATULATIONS
______________.
Your entry featuring the book
____
was judged
____
in the BOOK PARADE
on ______________.
____
signed

PARTICIPATION
AWARD!
Thank you, ____________,
for your entry in the BOOK
PARADE on ____________.
____
Signed

THANK YOU,
____________,
for judging our BOOK
PARADE on
____________.

WE'RE PARADING OUT THE BOOKS!

You're invited to view the BOOK PARADE!

Date ____________

Time ____________

Place ____________

Parent-gram

Your child's class will be participating in ________ School's Book Parade. The class has designed an entry based on the book

________________.

You are invited to attend!

Date:

Time:

Location:

____

Teacher

STORY
SPINNERS
A STORY SHARING
BOOK-A-BRATION!

STORY SPINNERS is an event designed to involve lower and upper grade students in books, reading and storytelling. It has many benefits such as:

- confidence for older students
- literature appreciation for younger students
- good PR for the library
- exposure of available books and materials

PLANNING & ORGANIZATION

1. Announce the event to the older students (see form on page 31). Ask for volunteers to read or tell stories to classes of younger children.

2. Sponsor a workshop for the volunteers. Show videos or let the students listen to recordings of storytellers. Display books with stories that are good for storytelling. Some students will be more comfortable reading a story. Have a selection of picture books for these students. If you have flannel board stories or puppets, you may wish to let the students choose from these as well. Talk to the students about voice and facial expression. Ask them to practice reading or telling stories in front of a mirror at home. You may want to have a follow-up workshop so the volunteers may practice with one another. Some students may like to visit their own classrooms to tell their stories, but chances are they'll be more comfortable with younger audiences. Encourage the students to be creative and dress like a character in the story if they wish.

3. Send an announcement to the teachers regarding the event (see page 32). Post a sign-up sheet in the library or lounge area for the teachers of the younger classes (see page 33). Sign-up should be voluntary. Clear the volunteers' participation with their teachers.

4. Divide the classrooms that have signed up for storytelling amoung the volunteers.

5. This may be a one-day, one-week, one-month or year-long event! Structure it as best suits your needs.

6. Give participation awards to the volunteers and send parent-grams home with the students (see page 36).

HEY KIDS!
Would you like to be a
STORY SPINNER?
The library is looking for volunteers to read and tell stories to primary classrooms.
An orientation workshop will be held on ________ at
(date)
______ in ____________.
(time)
(place)
* Volunteers must have the permission of their homeroom teachers.

THE LIBRARY IS PLEASED TO ANNOUNCE A STORY SPINNER CELEBRATION!

Several volunteer ___ graders are available to share books and stories with your classroom!

Date(s) available:

Time(s) available:

Sign-up information:

Teachers for grades ______________ may sign up below for a visit from a Story Spinner. You will receive a confirmation of the date and time.

CONFIRMATION
The following STORY SPINNER(S) will visit your classroom on ________ at ________:
____
____
to share the following:
____
____
ENJOY!
© 1990 by Incentive Publications, Inc., Nashville, TN.

STORY SPINNER MEMBERSHIP CARD
This is to certify that
____
is an official STORY SPINNER at ________
________.
Date
Signature
© 1990 by Incentive Publications, Inc., Nashville, TN.

Have each volunteer keep a record of the stories and books he or she shares by using this bookmark.

A story spinner badge for your volunteers to wear! (Color and laminate.)

Hint: If you are handy with a needle and thread, you might want to enlarge the spider emblem on this page and applique´ T-shirts for your volunteer story spinners!

THANKS!
for being a participant
in
STORY SPINNERS
Date
Signature
© 1990 by Incentive Publications, Inc., Nashville, TN.

PARENT-GRAM
Parents:
Just wanted to let you know
your child is a volunteer
STORY SPINNER
and is sharing books and stories
from our library with other classes!
Signature
© 1990 by Incentive Publications, Inc., Nashville, TN.

LIBRARY BOWL
1ST
ENCOURAGING & REINFORCING
STUDENTS IN LIBRARY AND
REFERENCE SKILLS.

THE LIBRARY BOWL is an academic competition intended to reinforce and recognize the achievement elementary students have made and are making in learning essential library and reference skills. It is a great way to get students more interested in these skills by providing them with a "culminating" event. It is also a great way to let teachers and parents know the library is on its toes!

PLANNING & ORGANIZATION

1. Send a flyer to every classroom announcing the Library Bowl. The flyers will explain what the Library Bowl is all about, which grades will be involved, and how many participants will be in the final competition. (Example: With a K-5 center, it works well to use fourth and fifth grades with two participants per room. Everyone may then be invited to view the Library Bowl.)

2. Use games and activities to help your students brush up on their library and reference skills during their library periods. You might have "library bees" (like spelling bees) by dividing the class into teams. This involves everyone and is a great activity...with no grades attached! Ask the students to respond orally to library and reference skills questions. Allow each student to have at least two misses before asking the student to be seated. Give the winner an award!

3. In order to generate more total involvement on the part of the students, post an incentive chart in the library. Each time a student turns in a correct skills work sheet, he or she receives a star. Give stars to the students who win skills games. Some games or work sheets are more difficult and should be worth two or three stars. Those students wanting to earn extra stars may visit a learning center and complete additional work. The two members of each class who receive the most stars should be chosen as the Library Bowl participants. (Important: It might be considered fair to take the top ten students overall, but choosing participants from each homeroom usually generates more interest.)

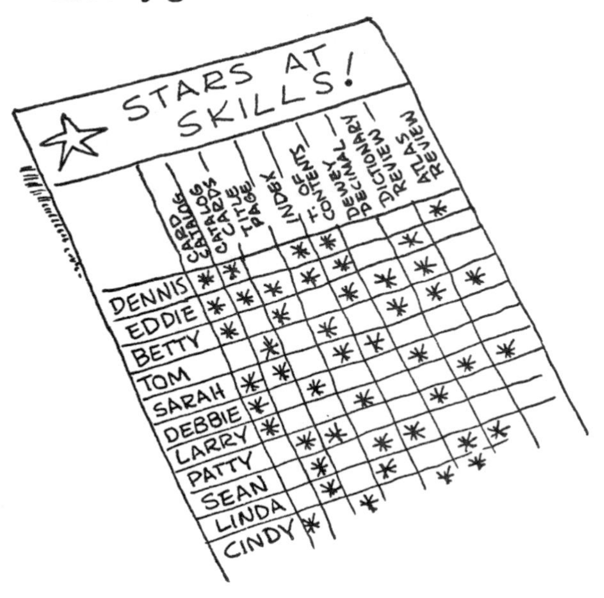

Not only does the incentive chart and star system narrow down the competition, but it also gets everyone excited and involved. Even those students who are not generally motivated, or those who do not feel they will be in the bowl, will work much harder when they realize that the class with the most stars will receive a pizza party or a movie based on a book! This way, every single star really does count! (Be sure to clear this with your principal.)

4. Have the question and answer list typed ahead of time! A suggested list of questions and answers may be found on pages 41 - 44. Have more questions than you think you will need! A safe bet is ten to fifteen questions per participating student. Be sure to make a copy of the questions and answers for each judge.

5. Secure judges. You will need a minimum of two or three. The judges should be other librarians from your district or public librarians from your community. (This is important when a student gives an answer that might be considered correct but is not strictly the answer on your sheet.) One judge should be the scorekeeper and timekeeper (he or she will need a stopwatch). Time should be called when a student has had ample time to reply.

6. Prepare the awards for the winners ahead of time. Certificates for all participants and winners may be found on pages 47 and 48. (Small engraved trophies can be purchased at a nominal cost.)

7. On the day of the library bowl. . .

- Seat the students and judges. Announce and introduce the Library Bowl. Give instructions to the participating students regarding the rules, time limits, etc.

- You may conduct the bowl in several ways. You may choose to have the students drop out after missing a specified number of questions (three, for example). Or, you may choose to keep all students in the competition and simply tally the points at the end of a time limit or number of rounds.

- Give awards to the students who place first, second and third (you may choose to give more awards depending on the number of participating students – see page 48). Be sure to give those who do not place participation awards (see page 47). Stress that each of the students involved has been a winner in knowledge and attitude!

- Thank your judges! Thank-you cards for the judges may be found on page 47.

- Be sure to have the press on hand to take pictures of the students!

NOTES:

- This program works best if you have a video camera. Students are generally not as nervous in a room with one camera as they are in a room with a large audience. The video can be viewed by individual classrooms or, if you have a closed circuit T.V. system, it can be aired to the entire school. Your other option is to have the library bowl in a gym or auditorium. If this is your choice, be sure to have a PA system.

- It is very likely that you will receive an added bonus by sponsoring the Library Bowl. Teachers always report how interested the students who observe the bowl are and how they answer the questions with the participants!

- It might be possible to get other librarians in your district interested in sponsoring library bowls at their schools. Then you could have a district-wide event after the individual school events!

SUGGESTED LIBRARY BOWL QUESTIONS

1. **Q.** Who is the person "responsible" for a book's pictures?
   A. Illustrator

2. **Q.** What is another name for the library?
   A. Media Center

3. **Q.** What are "made-up" stories called?
   A. Fiction

4. **Q.** The name of a book is its ________________ .
   A. Title

5. **Q.** What are "true" books or books of facts called?
   A. Nonfiction

6. **Q.** What does one call an alphabetical list of topics which gives the numbers of pages on which those topics may be found in that book?
   A. Index

7. **Q.** The person who writes a book is called the ______________ .
   A. Author

8. **Q.** Where in a book would one look to find out on what page a particular chapter begins?
   A. Table of contents

9. **Q.** A list of difficult or unusual words, and their meanings, used in a particular book is called a ____________________ .
   A. Glossary

10. **Q.** The "place" one looks to find a book in the library is the______________ .
    A. Card catalog

11. **Q.** Where is an index found in a book?
    A. At the back of the book

12. **Q.** Where is the table of contents found in a book?
    A. At the front of the book

13. **Q.** Where in a book would one find the glossary?
    A. At the back of the book

14. **Q.** What is the company called that publishes a book?
    A. Publisher

15. **Q.** What is the proper name for a book of maps?
    A. Atlas

16. **Q.** Another word for magazine is ____________________ .
    A. Periodical

17. **Q.** The story of a person's life is a ____________________ .
    A. Biography

18. **Q.** The story an author writes about his or her own life is an ____________________________ .
    A. Autobiography

19. **Q.** The page of a book on which one can find the title, author, publisher and copyright date is the ______________________ .
    A. Title page

20. **Q.** A special collection of books of facts used primarily for reports and looking up important information is the ________________________ .
    A. Reference section

21. **Q.** The year a book is published is called its ________________ .
    A. Copyright date

22. **Q.** What are the three types of catalog cards?
    A. Title, author, subject

23. **Q.** How can you tell what type of card a catalog card is?
    A. By looking at the top line of the card. Either the title, author or subject will be listed there. (The subject would be in all caps.)

24. **Q.** How are catalog cards arranged in the card catalog?
    A. Alphabetically, by the top line

25. **Q.** Flimstrips, videos and records are examples of what type of material?
    A. Audiovisuals

26. **Q.** By what system are nonfiction books classified?
    A. Dewey Decimal System

27. **Q.** Who invented the Dewey Decimal System?
A. Melvil Dewey

28. **Q.** How many classes are in the Dewey Decimal System?
A. Ten

29. **Q.** How are fiction books arranged on the shelf?
A. Alphabetically, by the author's last name

30. **Q.** How are biographies arranged on the shelf?
A. Alphabetically, by the last name of the person whom the book is about

31. **Q.** What do you call a book that contains stories about the lives of several different people?
A. Collective biography

32. **Q.** A collective biography is classified under what number of the Dewey Decimal System?
A. 920

33. **Q.** Folk tales and fairy tales are classified under what number of the Dewey Decimal System?
A. 398

34. **Q.** A reference book one might use to look up current information is an ______________________________ .
A. Almanac

35. **Q.** A reference book one might use to find the synonym for a word is a ____________________ .
A. Thesaurus

36. **Q.** What system is used to classify the reference section?
A. Dewey Decimal System

37. **Q.** Who began the first public library in America?
A. Benjamin Franklin

You may want to include some application questions. Place a book in front of the students for their reference and ask the following questions:

38. **Q.** Who is the author of this book?
39. **Q.** What is the name of the publisher of this book?
40. **Q.** Where was this book published?
41. **Q.** When was this book published?
42. **Q.** On what page does chapter three begin?

43. **Q.** How many pages does this book have?
44. **Q.** Does this book have an index? On what pages can the topic ______________ be found?

Place three numbered catalog cards in front of the students. Ask questions such as:

45. **Q.** What type of card is card no. ______ ?
46. **Q.** What is the title on card no. ______ ?
47. **Q.** Who is the author on card no. ______ ?
48. **Q.** What is the name of the publisher on card no. ______ ?
49. **Q.** How many pages are in the book ______________________ ?
50. **Q.** What is the call number of the book ____________________ ?
51. **Q.** What is the name of the illustrator of the book ___________________ ?

Prepare a page of spine labels with call numbers typed on them. Ask the students to answer questions such as:

52. **Q.** In what section of the library would number 4 be found?

Ask similar questions having the answers *reference, fiction, nonfiction, biography,* etc. Prepare a chart or display of audiovisual software and hardware (number each item). Ask the students to identify several numbered items.

DEWEY APPLICATION

53. **Q.** What is the classification name for the 500's?
    A. Pure Science
54. **Q.** What is the classification name for the 000's?
    A. General Works

Give book titles to the students. Ask the students to give the class name and number under which each book would be classified.

55. **Q.** A book of myths
    A. 200, Religion
56. **Q.** Know Your Government
    A. 300, Social Science
57. **Q.** Poems For Spring
    A. 800, Literature
58. **Q.** Rocks And Minerals
    A. 500, Pure Science
59. **Q.** The American Revolution
    A. 900, History
60. **Q.** Basketball Talk
    A. 700, Fine Arts and Recreation

HEY KIDS!

I'm proud of your efforts in learning library and reference skills this year!

A LIBRARY BOWL

for ___ participants in grade(s) ___________

will be held on _________!

* We will brush up on our skills with games and activities during your library period.

Work Hard!

PARENT - GRAM

STAR STUDENT

Congratulations!

Your child, ______________,
is a WINNER and will
be participating in the
LIBRARY BOWL

on ____________ at ________.
Date Time

You are invited to attend.

____
Librarian

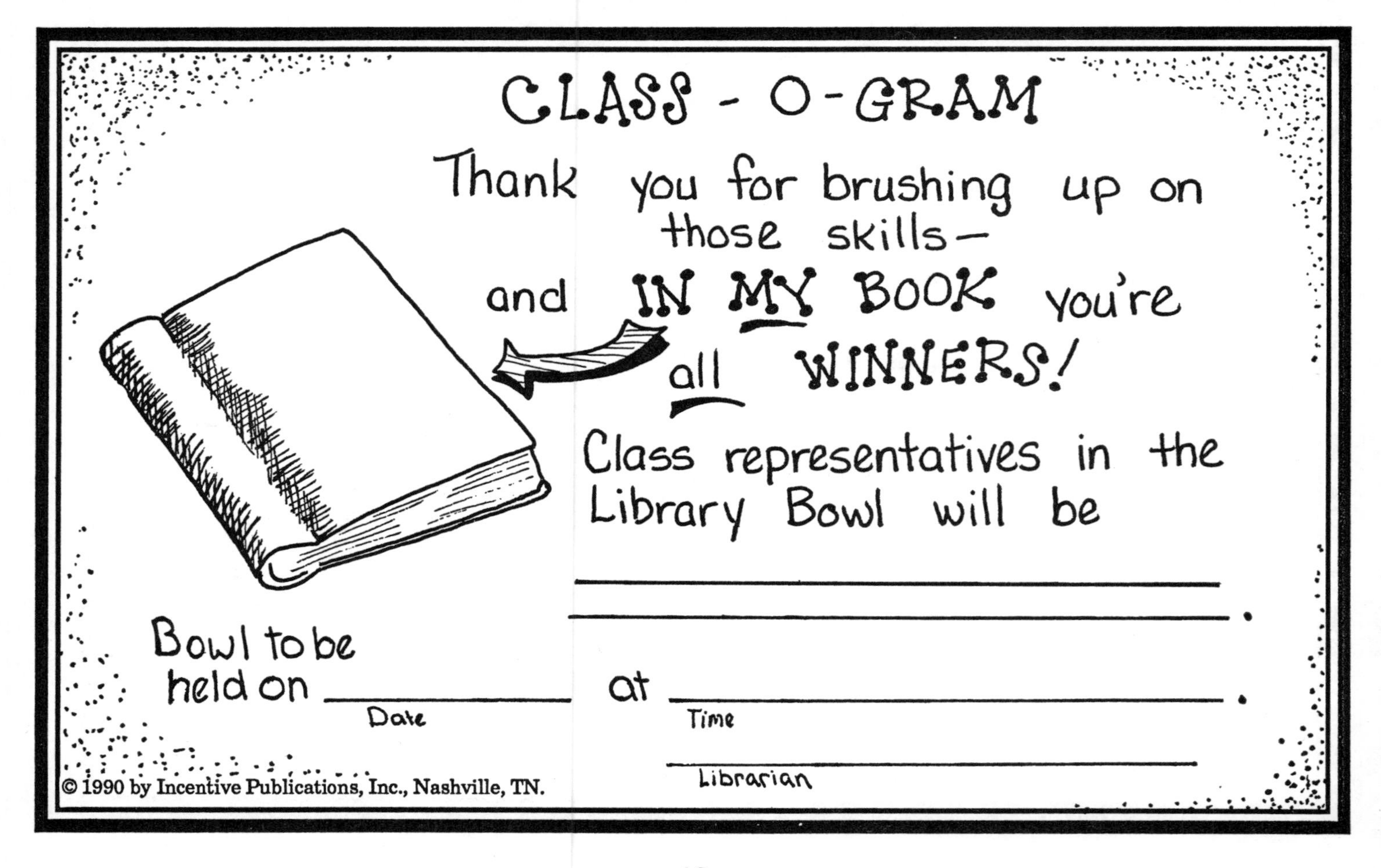

CLASS - O - GRAM

Thank you for brushing up on
those skills—
and IN MY BOOK you're
all WINNERS!

Class representatives in the
Library Bowl will be

____
______________________.

Bowl to be
held on ____________ at ______________.
Date Time

____
Librarian

THANKS,
________, for being a JUDGE in the LIBRARY BOWL!
Your time and interest were very appreciated!
School
Date
Librarian

Awarded to
name
for being a LIBRARY BOWL PARTICIPANT!
School
Date
Librarian
YOU'RE NO. 1
IN MY BOOK!

CONGRATULATIONS!
NAME
for placing in our
LIBRARY BOWL
at
SCHOOL
on
DATE
LIBRARIAN

LOVE THE BOOKS DAY
Feb. 14
* also known as: "I Love to Read Day"

LOVE THE BOOKS DAY is an excellent way to tie books and reading into a holiday celebration. This day is also celebrated in many libraries as "I Love To Read Day." In this section you'll find novel ideas for making Valentine's Day a day to "love the books" in *your* school!

- **BOOKMARKS** – Reproduce the bookmarks on page 51 and put one in each book checked out during the week of Valentine's Day.

- **RADIO SPOTS** and **INTERCOM ANNOUNCEMENTS** – See pages 52 - 54 for PR suggestions for your book-a-bration. Participation awards and parent-grams are included.

- **VALENTINE CONTEST** – Sponsor a contest in which the students make valentines for their favorite authors, illustrators, or book characters (see pages 55 - 58). An announcement, parent-gram and two awards are included.

- **BOOK ADOPTION** – Students who love books will love to adopt tattered books and repair them. See pages 59 - 61 for details.

- **VIDEO VALENTINE** – Videotape student representatives from each class as they give book talks about books they love. Ideas and forms for announcements, awards and parent-grams may be found on pages 62 - 64.

BOOKMARKS

for celebrating
LOVE THE BOOKS DAY

SUGGESTED SPOT ANNOUNCEMENT:

> "Love The Books Day" is being celebrated on February 14 at ______________ school. My name is ____________________. I'm in ____________'s class and I LOVE TO READ!

This announcement can be taped by representatives from each class and then aired on local radio stations (see "Radio Spots" – page viii). Or, a representative of each class may make this announcement intermittently throughout the day over the school intercom. (Be sure to get the principal's approval!)

For radio spots:

- Arrange for a local radio station to air the spots.
- Send an announcement to every class (page 53).
- Tape the class representatives as they read the "spot."
- Send parent-grams home with the students (page 54).
- Give the participants awards (page 54).

For intercom announcements:

- Check with the principal first.
- Send an announcement to every class (page 53).
- Send a schedule detailing when the students are to report to the office to the participating students.
- Send parent-grams home with the students (page 54).
- Give the participants awards (page 54).

________ representative(s) from each class are asked to come to the library on ____________________ at ____________________ to tape the announcement below for airing on local radio station ________________ the week of ______________________.

________ representative(s) from each class are asked to read the announcement below over the school intercom on "Love The Books Day," February 14. Your class representative(s) should report to the school office at ___________________.

ANNOUNCEMENT:

A Parent-Gram
JUST WANTED TO LET YOU KNOW THAT YOUR CHILD,
________________,
HELPED US CELEBRATE
Love the Books Day
AT ________________ BY
MAKING A SCHOOL INTERCOM ANNOUNCEMENT.
MAKING A RADIO SPOT. IT WILL AIR ON ______ THE WEEK OF ______.
SIGNED
© 1990 by Incentive Publications, Inc., Nashville, TN.

A BIG
HEARTFELT THANKS!
to
____
for helping ________ celebrate
Love the Books Day
with a special announcement!
© 1990 by Incentive Publications, Inc., Nashville, TN.

Bulletin Board Idea

A VALENTINE CONTEST in which students make valentines for favorite authors, illustrators and book characters is a creative way to entice students to share favorite books!

There are several ways to sponsor this program:

- Set up a table in the library, complete with papers, scissors, lace, glue, etc. Allow the students to make their own valentines.
- Send a flyer to classes announcing a "Win My Heart" contest (see page 56). Have different grade levels make different valentines. For example:

  K-1 valentines for favorite book characters
  2-3 valentines for favorite illustrators
  4-5 valentines for favorite authors

  If sponsoring a contest, it is best to have a winner for each grade level (awards on page 58). Give each student who participates a participation award (page 57) and display each and every valentine. Those that really "win your heart" might deserve a heart-shaped box of candy!

Hint: Suggest to the teachers that they make this a classroom art activity!

HEY KIDS!

THERE'S A CONTEST! DESIGN A VALENTINE FOR YOUR FAVORITE:

- ☑ AUTHOR
- ☐ ILLUSTRATOR
- ☐ BOOK CHARACTER

BE SURE TO WRITE A LITTLE ABOUT THE PERSON (?) YOUR VALENTINE IS FOR. TURN YOUR ENTRIES IN TO THE LIBRARY BY __________.

WINNERS ANNOUNCED ON _________.

All Valentines will be displayed, so do your best and

YOU COULD WIN MY HEART!

LOVED YOUR H'ART!

Thanks, ________,
for participating in
our
LOVE THE BOOKS
CELEBRATION
by making a valentine
for your favorite ______.

____
Librarian

Just wanted to let you
know that your child,
________,
FOUND THE WAY TO MY
HEART
by participating in our LOVE
THE BOOKS CELEBRATION and by
making a valentine for his/her
favorite ________.

____
Librarian

YOU'VE WON MY HEART!
CONGRATULATIONS, ________,
FOR PLACING ____ IN OUR
Valentine to Your Favorite
________ Contest
on ________ at ________.
DATE
SCHOOL OR LIBRARY
____
LIBRARIAN

ADOPT-A-BOOK is a wonderful program for students who would enjoy adopting a tattered and torn book to "spruce it up"! This will help reinforce book care as well as keep your collection in shape!

PREPARATION AND ORGANIZATION

1. Fill a table with books in need of care and post a sign announcing the program.

2. Give each child who participates a book adoption certificate (page 60).

3. Create a display of repair supplies such as tape, erasers, shelf or butcher paper, markers and scissors (for making new covers). Be sure to laminate or enclose the covers in plastic jackets.

4. Place a book plate inside each refurbished book so that others will know who was responsible for the book's "new look" (page 60). (This will make the participating students proud!)

5. Give a participation award to each student and send parent-grams home with the students (page 61).

BOOK ADOPTION CERTIFICATE

Congratulations, ______________!
You have officially adopted the book ______________ by __________.

You must:
- mend its torn pages.
- erase pencil marks.
- make a new cover for it.

Librarian ____________________

THIS BOOK'S PROUD GUARDIAN is

______________.

He/she repaired it, erased pencil marks, and made a new cover for it.

PLEASE TAKE CARE OF IT!

A BOOK PLATE FOR THE "NEW BOOK"!

THANKS,

______________,

for participating in the ADOPT-A-BOOK PROGRAM and adopting a book in need of care and attention.

Date ______________

Librarian ______________

Parent-Gram

Just wanted you to know how proud we are of __________, who participated in the ADOPT-A-BOOK PROGRAM by giving a tattered book a repair job and a sparkling new look!

Date ______________

Librarian ______________

VIDEO VALENTINE is a great way to get students involved in giving book talks and sharing favorite books. If your facility does not have access to a video camera, this idea can be adapted to live performances.

Each participating student is to give a book talk about a book that he or she "loves." You probably will need to explain the difference between a book talk and a book report. Limit the students' book talks to five minutes. Encourage each student to dress like a character from the book and tell about the book from the character's point of view. It is a good idea to give several book talks for the students during the preceding week.

PLANNING & ORGANIZATION

1. Decide how many representatives per class you wish to feature.

2. Send a flyer announcing the event to every class (see page 63). Classes may choose their representative(s) by drawing names, asking for volunteers, or holding class tryouts.

3. Post a sheet in the library or faculty lounge on which homeroom teachers may write the name(s) of their participant(s). This will give you a good idea of what to expect and how to plan.

4. Videotape the students and send an announcement regarding playback to every class. Although this works best if you have a closed circuit T.V. system, you may choose to air the video during library periods. Be sure to send parent-grams home with the students (see page 64) so that parents will know when they can view, too!

5. Give everyone who participates an award (see page 64)!

THE LIBRARY ANNOUNCES VIDEO VALENTINE

____ representative(s) from each classroom are asked to give a book talk on A BOOK THEY LOVE!

Book talks are limited to five minutes. Tell about a book you love and make others want to read it! Be creative and dress like a character from the book!

Representatives will be videotaped on ____________ at ________.
Report to __________ at that time.

Playback plans are: ______________
____

PARENT- GRAM
PARENTS:
Your child, ______,
is a star in
VIDEO VALENTINE,
a book review program.
It will air on ______
date
at ______.
time
You are invited to
come and view!
______
Librarian

THANKS
FROM THE BOTTOM
OF MY HEART!
for being a
participant in
VIDEO VALENTINE
on ______ at
date
______.
School
______
Librarian

READING
PROGRAMS

Bulletin Board Idea

THE BIG FISHERMAN READING CLUB can be done with a single class, a grade level or the entire school. It is a great spring pick-up that helps students catch the reading fever!

PLANNING & ORGANIZATION

1. Give each child who participates a "fishing-for-a-good-book" license (page 68) and a bookmark/reading record (page 70).

2. When each student finishes a book, he or she should write a mini-report on a construction paper fish (see page 69) and suspend the "catch" from a coat hanger with yarn. The student should write his or her name on a paper triangle and tape it to the coat hanger (see page 69).

3. The students' "catches" can be hung on a clothesline in the room.

4. Give each participant an award at the end of the program and send parent-grams home with the students (page 71).

5. Give the trophy "fish" (page 72) to the student who reads the most books!

ADDITIONAL IDEAS FOR A SUCCESSFUL PROGRAM

Tape paper "trees" to the wall.

Display books on a table labeled "The Pond" or "The Fishin' Hole"; or, if space allows, set up a reading corner.

Secure a section of fake "grass" for lounging and reading.

"Fill" a blue oilcloth "pond" with books.

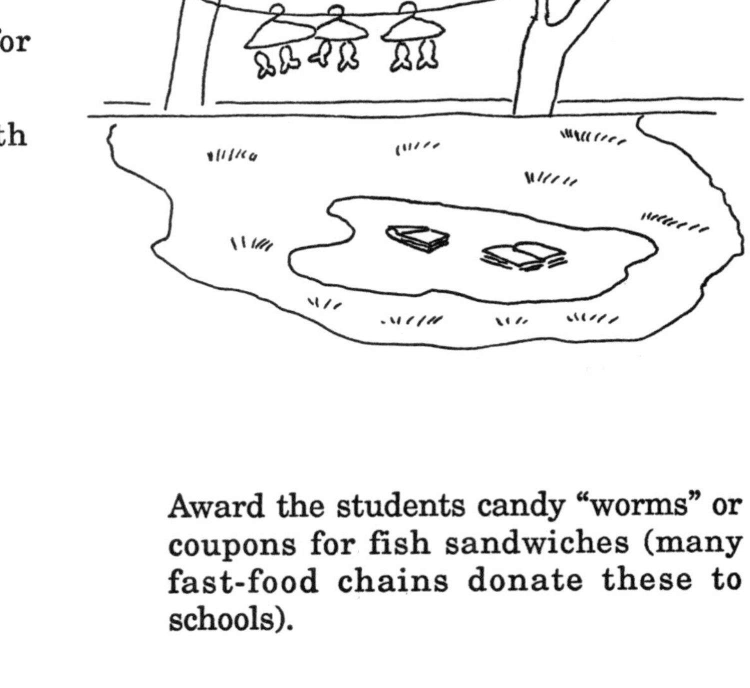

Award the students candy "worms" or coupons for fish sandwiches (many fast-food chains donate these to schools).

All fishermen love to tell tales! Have a sharing session and "swap stories"!

BAIT

A good book is

_______________.

YOU should read this book because

____

____

____

____

____

Student

Have the students fill out "bait" forms to entice others to read their favorite books. Display these in a can as shown.

FISH-FOR-A-GOOD-BOOK LICENSE

This certifies that _______________ is a member of the BIG FISHERMAN READING CLUB and is entitled to HOOK ALL THE GOOD BOOKS he/she can find!

Librarian _______________

Date _______________

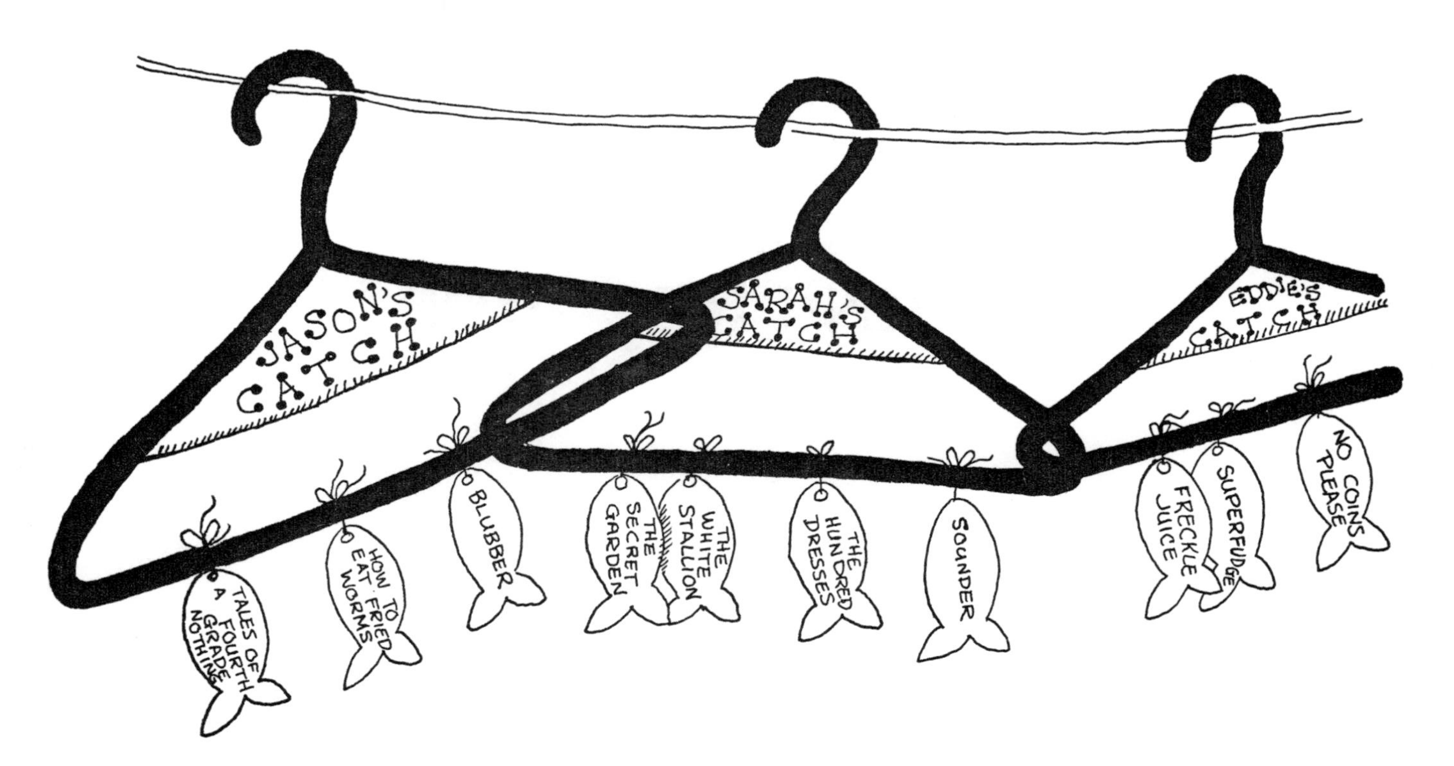

Suspend a clothesline in the classroom or library. Give each "fisherman" a coat hanger. Cover the top of the hanger with paper and write the "fisherman's" name on the paper. Have each student suspend his or her "catch" from the hanger when he or she completes a book.

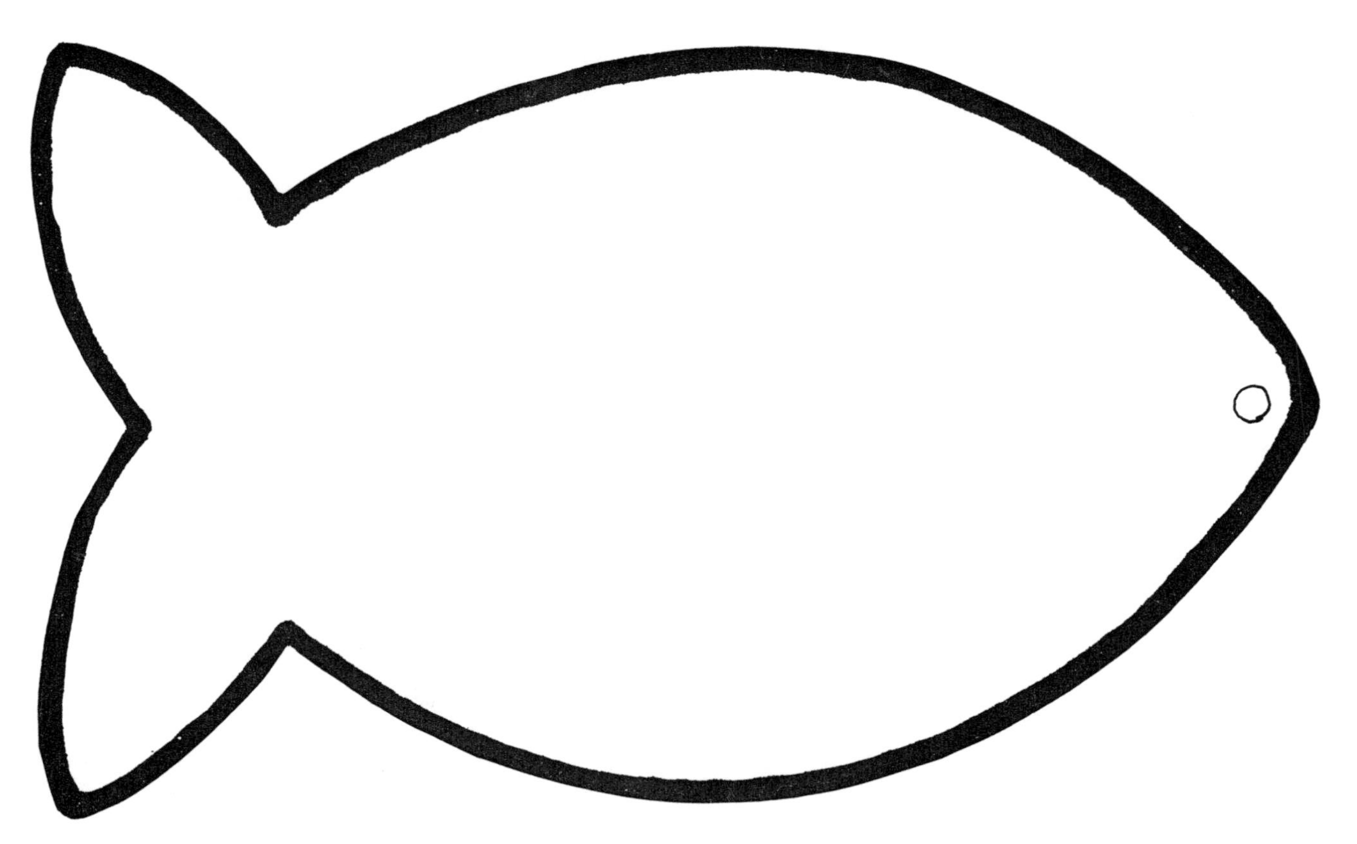

Cut "fish" out of bright colors of construction paper. Instruct each student to write a mini-report on one side and the title of the book on the other side.

BIG FISHERMAN BOOKMARKS/ READING RECORDS

SO GLAD YOU
CAUGHT ON
TO THE READING
SPIRIT
and read ___ books
in the BIG FISHERMAN
READING CLUB
at ___________.
School
Teacher / Librarian
Date

PARENT-GRAM
JUST "DROPPING YOU
A LINE" to let
you know that ___________
has successfully completed _____
books in the
BIG FISHERMAN READING
CLUB
at ___________.
School
Teacher/Librarian
Date

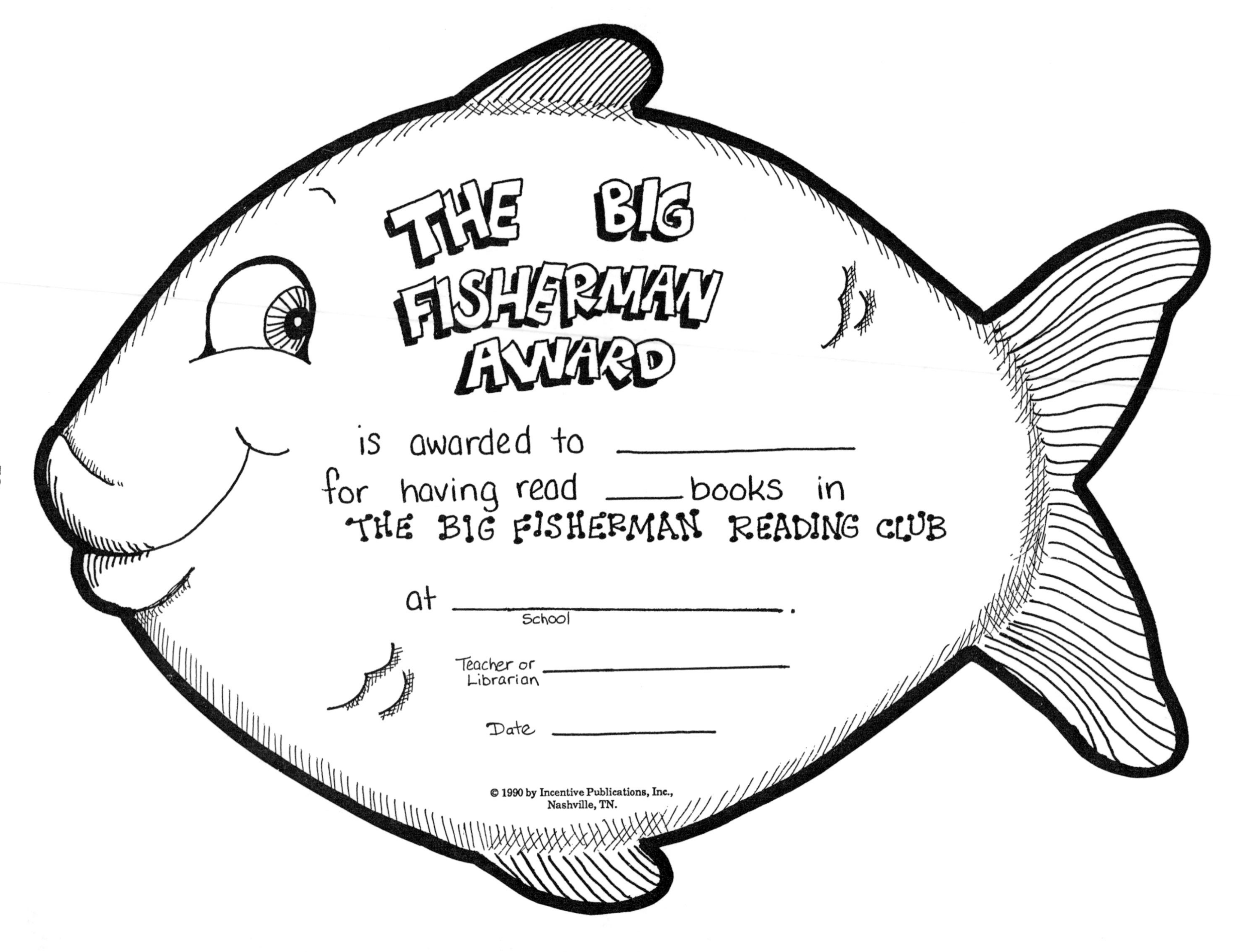
THE BIG FISHERMAN AWARD
is awarded to ____________
for having read ____ books in
THE BIG FISHERMAN READING CLUB
at ____________.
School
Teacher or Librarian ____________
Date ____________

Bulletin Board Idea

THE SMART COOKIES READING CLUB is a good program for any time of the year; however, it works very well as a December program as you can "tie in" the gingerbread men with the holiday season.

PREPARATION & ORGANIZATION

1. Give each student a membership card (page 75) and a bookmark (page 77).

2. As a student finishes a book, have him or her fill out a gingerbread man (page 76). (You may want to copy these on brown paper and add glitter for "icing.") Suspend the gingerbread men from the ceiling with yarn or use them to decorate a bulletin board.

3. Display cookie jars (page 74) for the participating rooms and label each jar with the teacher's name. As each student finishes a specified number of books, attach a "cookie" (a plain round sticker works well) with the student's name written on it to the jar.

4. Give each student a participation award and send parent-grams home with the students (page 78). A special award (page 79) goes to the student who reads the most books!

COOKIE JAR

Have each student fill out a "fortune cookie card" after reading an exceptionally good book. File these in a recipe box so that other readers may browse through them!

To make a great "hang-up," punch a hole in the gingerbread man and suspend it from the ceiling.

Copy the gingerbread man on brown paper and decorate it with glitter.

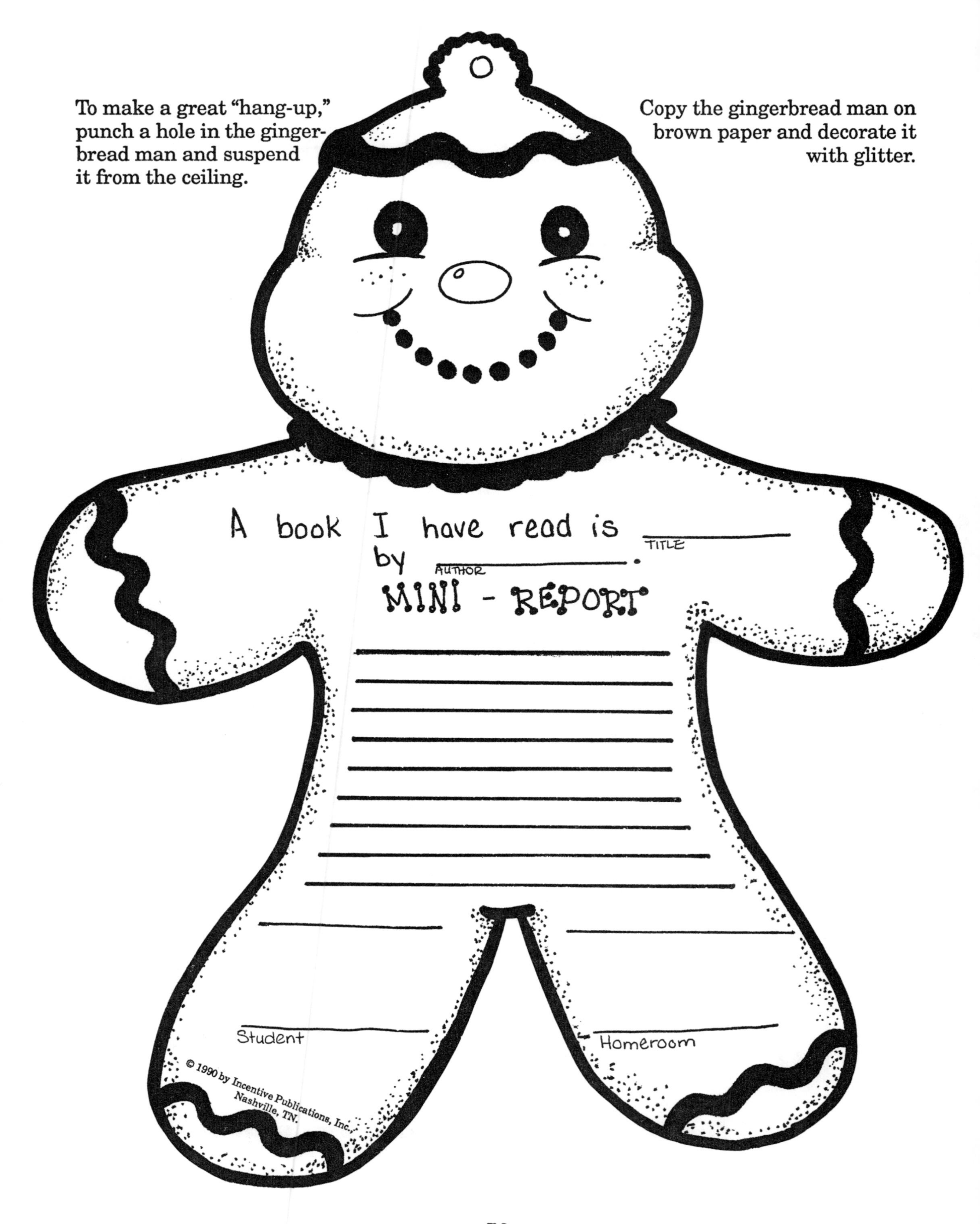

Display a cookie sheet and label it "smart cookies." To acknowledge those readers deserving special recognition, copy the pattern below on brown paper and decorate the gingerbread men with glitter. Then put a piece of magnetic tape on the back of each gingerbread man and display those "smart cookies"!

IT'S A
TREAT
to have
SMART COOKIES
who like to read!
Thanks, ________,
for participating in the
SMART COOKIES READING
PROGRAM
at ____________!
Date ________
Teacher or Librarian ________
COOKIE JAR
© 1990 by Incentive Publications, Inc., Nashville, TN.

PARENT - GRAM
Your child,
________,
is a SMART COOKIE
and has successfully
completed ___ books in
the SMART COOKIES
READING PROGRAM
at ________.
School / Library
Date
Librarian or Teacher
© 1990 by Incentive Publications, Inc., Nashville, TN.

SMART COOKIE
AWARD
to
for reading
books in the
SMART COOKIES
READING CLUB
at
School/Library
!
Date
Librarian